Introduction

Every day, my ministry reaffirms the fact that life is hard. While some people wish they could just "erase themselves," they have to keep going.

Troubles, heartaches, and problems are our constant companions. A cherished relationship ends; we close for the last time the eyes of someone we love; we're given a life-altering medical diagnosis; we're hurt by the unjust actions of others; we've lost faith in ourselves.

Some days you feel so far down in the pit, you can't function. No one can reach you. It's so overwhelming you can't catch your breath. Broken, you wonder: "Will I ever heal? Can I ever be happy again?" The good news is that you'll make it. Courage and happiness will return. Jesus is the one who will drop a rope down the pit—a rope with a huge knot at its end. "Don't look down," Jesus urges. "Look up. Hang on. Start climbing, knowing I'm right here beside you."

As you slowly but surely climb out of the pit, focus your eyes on Jesus. He's close to you, holding your hand and helping you dodge those tugs from below. He's empowering you to put one foot in front of the other and get on with life.

It's my wish that these Lenten reflections will be your lifeline to survive life's most difficult times so you can enjoy living again. Squeeze all you can out of these pages. My prayer is that, when Easter arrives, you will feel refreshed, rejuvenated, and ready to open your helping heart to hurting hearts all around you.

TWENTY-THIRD PUBLICATIONS A Division of Bayard; One Montauk Avenue, Suite 200; New London, CT 06320; (860) 437-3012 or (800) 321-0411; www.23rdpublications.com

ISBN 978-1-62785-054-4

Copyright ©2015 Joseph F. Sica. All rights reserved. No part of this publication may be reproduced in any manner without prior written permission of the publisher. Write to the Permissions Editor. Printed in the U.S.A.

FEBRUARY 18 | ASH WEDNESDAY

Joel 2:12–18 » 2 Corinthians 5:20—6:2 » Matthew 6:1–6, 16–18

Blindsided

"Go into your room, shut the door, and pray to your Father."
Matthew 6:6

Life has a way of taking us by surprise. One day, everything is swell, and then—BAM!—something sneaks up and knocks us senseless. It happened to me when I lost major heart function. While a considerable amount has returned, it carries with it some life-threatening complications. And it took months of cardiac rehab, a slew of medications, and, of course, changes in my diet.

What about you? Many things can derail us. A job loss due to the latest rounds of layoffs. A health crisis. An unexpected death. A happily-ever-after that didn't work out. It's easy to be thrown off course and left wondering whether or not we'll be able to get back up and move forward.

The good news is we can, and we will, as we enter Lent. All we need to do is reboot our inner GPS so we can get off the side of the road and get back on course. Let's face it—life doesn't always go according to plan. But with the right attitude, we can persevere through even the toughest situations. Don't check out on living life; check in stronger and better than ever. Maybe all you need is a change in your mental diet.

TAKEAWAY ROUTE: What has knocked you off course? Identify one small step you can take to bounce back. Sometimes, the smallest step is the most important.

TURN-IT-OVER ROUTE: *Jesus, help me get back on course whenever I lose my footing. Amen.*

FEBRUARY 19 | THURSDAY AFTER ASH WEDNESDAY

Deuteronomy 30:15–20 » Luke 9:22–25

Turn up the heat

"Follow me."

Luke 9:23

Voltaire once described a person as being a warming oven, always heating but never cooking. Many people live this way. Their lives are passion-impaired as they drag themselves through life without enthusiasm—heating just enough to get by without really cooking.

Jesus does not call us to simmer, but to boil, as he issues his irresistible directive—follow me. What soothing words for those who want to make a difference!

Simmering followers are complainers. "Follow Jesus? Get real! It can't be done." Lukewarm and lethargic, many of these followers fall into the "couldn't care less" category. If only we could bring them to a ferocious boil—from apathy to enthusiasm, from indifference to participation. Not only would they get more out of life, but imagine the impact they could have on others!

Boiling followers are fired up. They eagerly step into other people's worlds and infuse them with hope. Imitating Jesus, they reach out to those who are hurting, ignored, bullied, and lonely, speaking out about love, change, and second chances.

Are you simply simmering, or are you ready to boil over and use your gifts and abilities to change lives?

TAKEAWAY ROUTE: Is there a life you can heat up during Lent? An elderly friend? A struggling teenager? Knock on the door of a single mom or a new widow/widower and be the warming presence they need. Make a difference.

TURN-IT-OVER ROUTE: *Jesus, remind me that the only equipment I need to fire up a broken life is my own voice to speak soothing words. Amen.*

FEBRUARY 20 | FRIDAY AFTER ASH WEDNESDAY

Isaiah 58:1–9a » Matthew 9:14–15

Say it now!

"The days will come when the bridegroom is taken away."
Matthew 9:15

The real tragedy of life is not that it ends so soon, but that we wait too long to plunge into it. I listened as Rabbi Harold Kushner told this story: A priest was finishing the committal service at a cemetery. As the husband embraced his beloved's casket, he said, "Father, I loved my wife."

"I know you did," the priest responded.

The husband repeated, "Father, I loved my wife."

Hugging his parishioner, the priest again said, "I know you did."

A third time, he said, "Father, I loved my wife…and one day, I almost told her so."

Too often, we live as if we have unlimited time with those we love. But without warning, our lives can be turned upside down by illness, loss, or death. All we can do is look back with regret over putting off that well-rehearsed conversation with our parents, expressions of genuine concern for someone in need, time spent with our children, hospital visits with loved ones, or, like the bereaved husband in the above story, simply saying the words "I love you."

Every day, we're given the opportunity to embrace special moments. Since we have such a limited time, we need to make that time count. Don't wait to tell your family and friends how you feel. Do it today.

TAKEAWAY ROUTE: Be still and ask what opportunities of love you are letting slip away. Then listen…and act.

TURN-IT-OVER ROUTE: *Jesus, when opportunity knocks, help me to answer the door. Amen.*

FEBRUARY 21 | SATURDAY AFTER ASH WEDNESDAY

Isaiah 58:9b–14 » Luke 5:27–32

The squeaky wheel

The Pharisees and scribes were complaining.
Luke 5:30

A monk joined a monastery, taking a vow of silence. After the first ten years, his superior asked him: "Do you have anything you'd like to say?"

The monk replied, "Food bad."

After another ten years, the monk again had the opportunity to voice his thoughts. "Bed hard."

A decade passed, and again he was summoned by his superior.

"I quit."

"It doesn't surprise me a bit," his superior responded. "You've done nothing but complain since you got here."

We all know someone who consistently whines. Working and living with a constant complainer can drain us emotionally.

To avoid participating in a grumble-a-thon, distance yourself by spending as little time as possible with them. While this isn't always an option, challenge the whiner by asking, "What are you going to do about it?" Don't be surprised if they get huffy and walk away. When you call them out on their complaining nature and ask them to take responsibility, they're often unwilling to accept the call to action. Just offer your best Cheshire cat smile. There's nothing like a little conviction to drive a person crazy!

TAKEAWAY ROUTE: Nobody likes to be the sounding board for chronic complainers. What do you do to keep the bellyachers at bay?

TURN-IT-OVER ROUTE: *Jesus, you are so amazingly patient with me even when I lapse into my complaining mode. Turn my whining into worship. Amen.*

FEBRUARY 22 | **FIRST SUNDAY OF LENT**

Genesis 9:8–15 » 1 Peter 3:18–22 » Mark 1:12–15

Breaking ground

"Repent, and believe in the good news."
Mark 1:15

"Fred, what are you looking for?" his friend asked as Fred foraged on the street on his hands and knees.

"I lost my house key."

"Oh, that's terrible. I'll help you look." He joined the search for the lost key. "About where did you lose it?"

"I lost it in my house," Fred responded.

"Then why are we looking out here?"

Fred replied, "Because there's more light here."

What's essential is not out in the light—it's buried inside you, where it can be frightening and dark. Pick up the shovel and begin to excavate and dig out that which is keeping you from thriving. Delve into the heart of who you are, and you'll see exactly what it is that is holding you back.

Be prepared, however. Excavation is not for the faint of heart. There's bound to be a showdown with some things that aren't serving you well. Challenges in parenting and relationships. Paralyzing fears and career obstacles. Self-doubt, lack of motivation, uncertainty. But keep digging! Eventually, you'll hit the wellspring of authentic living in relationship with yourself, others, and God. It's bubbling up. All you have to do is dig.

TAKEAWAY ROUTE: Place a toy shovel in the place where you pray as a reminder to dig…deep. Throughout Lent, look at your relationships with yourself, God, family, friends, and those you don't yet know very well.

TURN-IT-OVER ROUTE: *Jesus, help me dig through the rubble in my life and make the necessary changes so I can hear your voice. Amen.*

FEBRUARY 23 | MONDAY OF THE FIRST WEEK

Leviticus 19:1–2, 11–18 » Matthew 25:31–46

A spark of kindness

"Just as you did it to one of the least of these who are members of my family, you did it to me." Matthew 25:40

The comments hurt. You look different. You aren't as talented, attractive, fit, or intelligent as those around you. They mock you, and it hurts. Let's face it: unkindness repels, whereas kindness attracts.

Kindness can be experienced in the small things we do—listening when another person is talking, avoiding being caught up in the rumor mill, and supporting rather than laughing at someone.

God has already provided us with everything we need to use kindness to ease another's burdens. Just one small act goes a long way: a gentle hug, a personal note, a phone call, or a simple text message of prayer and support. Providing a meal or running an errand for someone in pain can turn their day around.

Every act of kindness begets kindness, creating a ripple effect that can turn the tide for someone else. We experience this every time we spotlight other people's strengths rather than their weaknesses, refuse to participate in hurtful gossip, step back and let someone else take center stage, or simply let them share their story without interrupting and correcting them. The Dalai Lama reminds us to "be kind whenever possible. It's always possible."

TAKEAWAY ROUTE: Throughout the week, write, call, or text someone whose kindness has had a significant impact on your life.

TURN-IT-OVER ROUTE: *Jesus, help me remember that one spark of kindness can set the world on fire. Amen.*

FEBRUARY 24 | TUESDAY OF THE FIRST WEEK

Isaiah 55:10–11 » Matthew 6:7–15

Fill the prescription

"Forgive us our debts, as we also have forgiven our debtors."
Matthew 6:12

How many times have you awakened with a sore jaw from grinding your teeth? Perhaps you are nursing a grudge. When the simple mention of someone's name sets your stomach churning, chances are good that a bit of forgiveness is needed. Still not sure? Check your mood meter. Does speaking their name flood you with anger, bitterness, hatred, and resentment? Who is it? A controlling mother? Demanding father? Deceitful spouse? Envious friend? Do you really want to carry this with you forever—whether you choose to speak to them or not?

Life is way too short to waste subscribing to past experiences, fueling animosity, registering wrongs, and harboring unhealthy emotions. There is a wonderful ring to the word "forgiveness." It is an action word suggesting a release. It's soothing and healing, reuniting those once torn apart. Forgiveness is an acceptance of the humanity in you and me.

Is it time for your annual checkup? Listen to the Great Physician and take some forgiveness "antibiotics." Let them cure the resentment infecting your soul. It won't be immediate, but in time you'll be on the road to recovery—with peace as the outcome.

TAKEAWAY ROUTE: Lent is an appropriate time to let go of the grudge you've been harboring for awhile…maybe even years. Write it out, bury it, and forget about it.

TURN-IT-OVER ROUTE: *Jesus, I'm hurt and I don't understand why this was done to me. Soften my heart with forgiveness so I don't have to carry this burden any longer. Amen.*

FEBRUARY 25 | WEDNESDAY OF THE FIRST WEEK

Jonah 3:1–10 » Luke 11:29–32

I can see clearly now

"The people of Nineveh will rise up at the judgment with this generation and condemn it." Luke 11:32

"Her laundry isn't very clean," Ann told John, looking out the kitchen window as her new neighbor hung her wash on the line. "She needs a lesson on how to wash her clothes."

John continued to read his newspaper in silence. Every time the neighbor hung out her wash, Ann would repeat her criticism and John would remain silent.

A few weeks later, Ann was surprised to look out of her window to discover a fresh row of radiantly clean laundry. Shocked, she commented, "Look, she finally learned how to do her wash, and I never even said a word."

John looked up from his paper. "No, she didn't do anything different, Ann. I just finally washed our windows this morning."

Sound familiar? Rather than gazing out of your own dirty windows, be a recovering judge-aholic. When the temptation comes to pass judgment on someone, firmly say to yourself, "Stop it!" People are different. They are not perfect. They do things that annoy, anger, and disappoint, so we all need to focus on our own laundry before we go about judging someone else's.

TAKEAWAY ROUTE: Print out some stickers that say: Don't judge me because I sin differently than you. Hand them out to those who aren't yet in recovery.

TURN-IT-OVER ROUTE: *Jesus, help me to never look down on anyone—unless I plan to help them up. Amen.*

FEBRUARY 26 | THURSDAY OF THE FIRST WEEK

Esther C:12, 14–16, 23–25 » Matthew 7:7–12

Who needs a love transfusion?

"Ask, and it will be given you."
Matthew 7:7

"Let me know if there is anything I can do to help." In the midst of the unimaginable, those words from friends and family are a balm to our battered souls. When plunged into an emotionally difficult situation like addiction, job layoff, divorce, depression, or the death of a loved one, we need to know we are not alone. When bleeding this way, we are desperately in need of a love transfusion.

Hurting people are all around us. Some wear plastic masks, disguising scarred souls. Show up for them. To be available is not talk; it's action. Be there so the wounded person will feel safe to disclose their pain, trusting that you won't brush it off, joke with them, change the subject, or spout off Bible verses or religiously oriented platitudes. Be a shoulder they can cry on. Lend an ear and truly listen. Hand them tissues to wipe their tears. Watch their children. Pick up groceries and cook. Walk their dog. Skip the simplistic answers to their crisis, grief, tragedy, or loss.

Be present but not pushy. Respect their space and need for isolation as they struggle to make sense of what has happened.

TAKEAWAY ROUTE: Hugging is a miracle drug. Look for overworked, overdrawn, overlooked, overwrought people and give 'em a squeeze.

TURN-IT-OVER ROUTE: *Jesus, help me recognize those who are hurting around me. Amen.*

FEBRUARY 27 | FRIDAY OF THE FIRST WEEK

Ezekiel 18:21–28 » Matthew 5:20–26

The elephant in the room

"First be reconciled to your brother or sister."
Matthew 5:24

The shouting grows louder, both sides convinced they are right. Since neither will back down, one shuts down, and the other walks away.

Are you ready for some real change? Sit across from each other face-to-face and eliminate any distractions. One person speaks on Monday. The other can only listen and try to perceive the world through the other's eyes without speaking. They get their chance on Tuesday, without the other's input. On Wednesday, after the words and feelings have marinated, both discuss practical ways to repair the relationship.

Here are some guidelines. Always:

Accentuate the positive. Do not criticize. Mention what you admire, prize, or cherish about the other person.

Ask for needs. "I need you to be sensitive to the way you talk to me." "I need you to stop lying." "I need affection."

Allow the other person to be who they are, complete with choices, personality, and feelings that they contribute to the relationship. Freely express emotions of hurt, anger, disappointment, intimidation, and insult. Add thoughtfulness, consideration, and romance—all expressions of love motivating you to work toward a resolution in mending the relationship.

TAKEAWAY ROUTE: Hesitant to have that talk? Don't leave it unsaid. Get it out. Make the necessary adjustments and move forward.

TURN-IT-OVER ROUTE: *Jesus, help me to talk compassionately and listen deliberately so my relationships can be stronger and healthier. Amen.*

FEBRUARY 28 | SATURDAY OF THE FIRST WEEK

Deuteronomy 26:16–19 » Matthew 5:43–48

Difficult? Who, me?

"He makes his sun rise on the evil and on the good, and sends rain on the righteous and on the unrighteous."
Matthew 5:45

What do the following have in common: the bold and blunt who intimidate, schemers lurking to sabotage, crybabies, people who bowl others over, and accusers full of insinuations? They're all difficult.

Difficult people come in many shapes and sizes. We all face them. Maybe it's your ex, your parents or in-laws, your employer, employees, or coworker. Sometimes it's the store cashier, the customer service agent, or another customer. It can even be your own children. They rub us the wrong way, push our buttons, and drive us up the wall. Unfortunately, when we confront them, our reaction is not always a pleasant one.

Whenever a difficult person wanders into your life, don't take it personally. Imagine them wearing a button that says, "It's not you. I'm nasty to everyone." Before resentment piles up and tempers start to flare, take a deep breath, think, and respond with confidence. Firmly remind them that while their behavior may be acceptable to others, it's not with you. Express what is expected, including the consequences.

Practice navigating interactions and disengage effectively. Avoid being sucked into their difficult behavior cycle, and take heart!

TAKEAWAY ROUTE: Do others consider you difficult? Ask yourself: Am I judgmental, inattentive, or negative? Am I a whiner or complainer? Am I touchy, intolerant, or aggressive? If yes, sit with a trusted friend and develop positive steps toward improving yourself throughout Lent.

TURN-IT-OVER ROUTE: *Jesus, if I'm going to love difficult people, I need your help so that my love will be real and not the fake stuff. Amen.*

MARCH 1 | SECOND SUNDAY OF LENT

Genesis 22:1–2, 9a, 10–13, 15–18 » Romans 8:31b–34 » Mark 9:2–10

Ch-ch-ch-changes

He did not know what to say, for they were terrified.
Mark 9:6

How we deal with the curve balls life throws at us makes a difference. Life-changing moments happen to each of us. Some we choose—weddings, careers, starting families, or moving. It's the other events that haunt us—those we're thrust into without choice or warning. None of us are immune to individual crises, whether it's a loved one's death, a tidal wave of unexpected expenses, illness, addiction, divorce, or job loss. All rock our world and knock us off-balance. This can't be happening, we think. We refuse to believe it. The thought of what's happening haunts our every waking hour.

Having experienced life-changing moments firsthand, I've learned we're not born with super-human resilience that insulates us from pain. Every transformational experience is an opportunity to dig deeper into ourselves and access resources we didn't know we had. Inevitably, there are lessons learned through this that are necessary for acquiring wisdom. We just have to search for them.

Your life-changing moment is neither good nor bad; it just is. Whether it makes you or breaks you is determined by the way you interpret it and respond. Embrace these life transformations as times pregnant with opportunities…opportunities to learn, to change, and to grow.

TAKEAWAY ROUTE: Every story of success is also a story of triumph over adversity. What story are you writing?

TURN-IT-OVER ROUTE: *Jesus, whatever comes my way, you are first on my speed dial. Together we will work it out. Amen.*

MARCH 2 | MONDAY OF THE SECOND WEEK

Daniel 9:4b–10 » Luke 6:36–38

What goes around, comes around

"The measure you give will be the measure you get back."
Luke 6:38

Have you ever thought about boomerangs? They soar into the sky and then curve to return to the thrower. Skillful throwers can heave them more than one hundred yards and back again, crossing through the air close enough to be caught by hand. Florence Scovel Shinn writes: "The game of life is a game of boomerangs. Our thoughts, actions, and words return to us sooner or later with astonishing accuracy."

Someone brought to their knees by recent news—their breath stolen, their resolve depleted—is badly in need of a boomerang helpout. It says, "I'm here. How can I help?"

Because we ourselves have been banged about and bruised, it's easy to open our arms to someone who is hurting and offer our help in practical ways. Go beyond saying "I understand"; roll up your sleeves and do something. A simple meal or an offer to drive somewhere can transform someone's day. Maybe you just need to hold out the bucket and allow the wounded person to fill it up with their needs. Replace the needs with solutions whenever possible. A boomerang helpout smoothes many a bumpy road.

TAKEAWAY ROUTE: Avoid clichés like "Time heals all sorrow" or "He'd want you to be strong" or "She wouldn't want you to be sad." Put away the clichés and pull out the compassion.

TURN-IT-OVER ROUTE: *Jesus, when my heart is shattered, thank you for the boomerang helpouts that show up to put it back together. Amen.*

MARCH 3 | TUESDAY OF THE SECOND WEEK

Isaiah 1:10, 16–20 » Matthew 23:1–12

Getting back on track

"They tie up heavy burdens…and lay them on the shoulders of others."
Matthew 23:4

"I feel demoralized," Janet told me. "He's always finding fault with me. Over the years, I feel beaten up by it all."

Janet isn't alone in her feelings. Too often, relationships are derailed by destructive behaviors that endanger our human dignity. Growth is stunted with insensitivity to each other's needs.

By contrast, when a relationship is on track, the ride is fun. You never want it to end. Of course, it takes work to keep it on track. Without continual maintenance, any relationship can run into trouble.

Through the years of hearing couples describe their relationships as train wrecks, I've noticed it's rarely the big problems knocking them off track. Instead, it's a series of small, inconsiderate behaviors, thoughtless comments, words left unspoken, or loving actions left undone.

Relationships wither slowly, starved by a lack of proper nurturing. In order to thrive, we need to be willing to put the time and attention into our relationships, providing regular maintenance and occasional tune-ups full of tenderness, forgiveness, and love. Don't allow laziness to derail you.

TAKEAWAY ROUTE: Put a small box in your kitchen to serve as a cell phone depot. While dining with family and friends, ask everyone to silence their phones and place them in the box. Then enjoy a distraction-free dinner focusing on what's important—the people gathered around the table.

TURN-IT-OVER ROUTE: *Jesus, in my relationships, it shouldn't always be about me. Help me to pay attention to those around me. Amen.*

MARCH 4 | WEDNESDAY OF THE SECOND WEEK

Jeremiah 18:18–20 » Matthew 20:17–28

Setting boundaries

"Declare that these two sons of mine will sit, one at your right hand and one at your left, in your kingdom." Matthew 20:21

"Unless I'm doing everything according to her way, my mom gets upset with every detail of my wedding plans," a young bride-to-be shared with me. Another woman said, "My mom shows up at my home and starts rearranging the furniture." Moms are full of love, kindness, and support, yet they can be smothering, nagging, and more than a bit pushy. It's not healthy when parents exert constant pressure on their children to be cookie-cutter versions of themselves. When they become overly involved—choosing your friends, college, wardrobe, etc.—problems are inevitable and well-defined boundaries are a necessity.

Drawing a line in the sand will help prevent a parent from running your life. You are no longer an infant—you're an adult, fully capable of making responsible decisions. But first you have to stop the meddling. Be truthful, clear, and direct. Tell your mom or dad what they're doing, how it makes you feel, and what changes need to be made.

They may try using the guilt card, but stand your ground. Otherwise, nothing will change. Try to ignore the cries, insults, and threats as he or she clearly disregards your opinions. Guard yourself against being equally as insulting, or you'll ruffle even more feathers.

TAKEAWAY ROUTE: Schedule a sit-down with your mom or dad. Be polite but firm. Share that, despite their good intentions, this just isn't working for you.

TURN-IT-OVER ROUTE: *Jesus, give me the courage to speak out to those who keep prying into my life. Amen.*

MARCH 5 | THURSDAY OF THE SECOND WEEK

JEREMIAH 17:5–10 » LUKE 16:19–31

An impartial friend

"No, father Abraham; but if someone goes to them from the dead, they will repent." LUKE 16:30

By the time his wife and son arrived at the emergency room, he was already dead. As his wife went into shock, the little boy shook his father and cried, "Daddy, wake up. Please wake up. We're supposed to go fishing tonight." Earlier that day, his father had told his boss he didn't feel well—and then he passed out. When the paramedics arrived, cardiac arrest had claimed his life, and it was too late.

A sudden death or diagnosis of a fatal illness causes many of us to reflect on the wonder of life, viewing death as a villain. I personally have made peace with death. I see it as Mark Twain did—"the only impartial friend I have." It lets me know I have a limited amount of time, and it doesn't deceive. It's never hidden itself from us.

Too often, we put things off. We plan to do them when our schedules open up. The time to do the things we want is now because tomorrow may never get here. Don't wait until someone's in hospice to say "I love you." Do it now! Value every moment as if it were your last. Live it, because it might very well be.

TAKEAWAY ROUTE: Whether it's wacky, wild, fearless, or frivolous, compile a list of things you want to do or see before you die—or grow too old to enjoy.

TURN-IT-OVER ROUTE: *Jesus, when I wake up, help me look out the window—of opportunities—and embrace them, wasting no time. Amen.*

MARCH 6 | FRIDAY OF THE SECOND WEEK

Genesis 37:3–4, 12–13a, 17b–28a » Matthew 21:33–43, 45–46

Don't putter with your clutter

"This is the heir; come, let us kill him and get his inheritance."
Matthew 21:38

"I'm a hoarder," Rose confessed. "I have rooms full of things I need to get rid of, but every time I walk through them, I find an excuse not to toss things." Who lives like that? We all do to some extent. We may not be hoarder-caliber messy, but there is clutter in our lives. And we need to cut it.

People's lives can overflow with stuff. We're hungry for new things, and we're attached to the things we have. Some even rent space to hold it. Clutter may seem trivial to some, but it defines happiness for others. Outer order really can create inner peace.

Begin a purge by doing a walk-through of your rooms, closets, garage, attic, basement, and drawers of your home. Create piles of items you don't need—giveaway pile, sell pile, and throwaway pile. Have a garage sale, or list items on Craigslist. Go through every space and take no prisoners! The hard part is getting started, but once you do, you won't want to stop. You'll be surprised how easy it is to navigate from room to room without ever stubbing your toes!

TAKEAWAY ROUTE: When clearing out your clutter, follow the OHIO Rule (Only Handle It Once). When you're done, create a "relaxation room," keeping only the minimum amount of stuff in it.

TURN-IT-OVER ROUTE: *Jesus, give me the energy and motivation to simplify my life and keep it that way. Amen.*

MARCH 7 | **SATURDAY OF THE SECOND WEEK**

Micah 7:14–15, 18–20 » Luke 15:1–3, 11–32

Tongue-tied

"Father, I have sinned against heaven and before you."
Luke 15:18

"I really didn't mean to hurt you," Andy said to his wife, Margaret, after she found some e-mails to his former girlfriend. "I was just lonely." This kind of halfhearted apology prevents Andy from taking full responsibility for his action and leaves Margaret feeling he's being insincere. It implies she is somehow responsible for his inappropriate behavior. Andy may have felt they were growing apart, so he reached out to his ex-girlfriend. A better choice would have been to sit down and talk with Margaret and share his feelings—in front of a marriage counselor, if necessary. A straightforward apology was needed.

For many of us, saying "I'm sorry" is a painful admission of fault. It leaves us feeling vulnerable. Pride, or just downright stubbornness, prevents us from saying it, further straining the relationship and preventing it from being salvaged and restored. The result? Lifelong grudges and bitter vengeance.

However, being able to say "I was out of line" is a sign of strength, not weakness. Saying "I'm sorry" is far better than saying "I didn't mean it." Our ability to apologize shows we are sensitive to the pain of others and offers the possibility of reconciliation.

TAKEAWAY ROUTE: If you're holding in an unexpressed apology, try writing these words: *[person's name)], I'm sorry for [name the hurt you caused].* Practice reading this over and over. Then tear up the paper and go apologize face-to-face.

TURN-IT-OVER ROUTE: *Jesus, help me loosen my tied tongue so I can say to those I hurt, "I'm sorry." Amen.*

MARCH 8 | THIRD SUNDAY OF LENT

Exodus 20:1–17 » 1 Corinthians 1:22–25 » John 2:13–25
or (Year A) Exodus 17:3–7 » Romans 5:1–2, 5–8 » John 4:5–42

The power of our words

Many Samaritans from that city believed in him because of the woman's testimony. John 4:39

"Sticks and stones can break my bones, but words will never hurt me." Do you remember this saying from when you were young? I sure do. But you know what? It's not true.

Words can conjure up powerful emotions. They can hurt or heal, build up or tear down, discourage or inspire. Words can make us laugh or cry, bring comfort or curse. Once said, words can never be taken back.

Those little put-downs can leave emotional scars on their victims. Calling someone "dumb," "ugly," or "a loser" can do lasting damage.

When relationships are at stake, it's essential to choose words that empower. We can boost someone's confidence with an encouraging word. Speak like Jesus did with the woman at the well. By speaking the truth while accepting her, making her feel valued and loved, Jesus empowered her to spread the good news.

Of course, we all slip on occasion. When you do, acknowledge it. Apologize. Move on. God has given us two ears and one mouth. Can you imagine the trouble we would be in if it were the other way around? Mother's advice still holds true: "If you can't say anything nice, don't say anything at all."

TAKEAWAY ROUTE: When was the last time you actually thought about what you say? It's time to seriously do a word-check and recreate a new language of love, positivity, gratitude, and humility.

TURN-IT-OVER ROUTE: *Jesus, may my words always be gentle, helping others to heal and grow. Amen.*

MARCH 9 | MONDAY OF THE THIRD WEEK

2 Kings 5:1–15b » Luke 4:24–30

Toss me an anchor

"No prophet is accepted in the prophet's hometown."
Luke 4:24

The saying "Don't get your hopes up" was familiar to Eileen, a single mother. She was told she had only thirty days to buy the house she lived in; otherwise, she would be evicted. On that same day, on the other side of town, another woman decided to call her just to say hello. That one call changed both of their lives forever.

"It was apparent she had been crying," the caller explained, "so she told me about the eviction. I knew that what happened to them could happen to any of us." Together, they hatched a plan to save the family home.

Do get your hopes up. Hope is in the house and it has a name—Jesus. He connected with people whose lives were at an all-time low, with the paralyzed, marginalized, and possessed, with all who were hanging on by a thread and ready to let go. Jesus entered their world and said, "Don't you dare give up! Anchor yourself in me and connect with others."

Jesus urges each of us to be a hope-bringer. Hope looks for the good in people, lifts discouraged spirits, energizes the overworked, and reminds us that God is still in control even in the worst of times. Hope points to the light at the end of the tunnel of misery.

TAKEAWAY ROUTE: Do you know someone who's ready to give up? Reach out and say, "I care. Want to talk about it?"

TURN-IT-OVER ROUTE: *Jesus, when I'm anchored in hope, I can hold fast through the fierce storms of life. Amen.*

MARCH 10 | TUESDAY OF THE THIRD WEEK
DANIEL 3:25, 34–43 » MATTHEW 18:21–35

Paying attention to one heart at a time

"And out of pity for him, the lord of that slave released him and forgave him the debt." MATTHEW 18:27

Four-year-old Nicholas saw his elderly, recently widowed neighbor crying, so he went over to his porch, climbed onto his lap, and just sat there. When his mother asked him what he had said to the neighbor, Nicholas said, "Nothing. I just helped him cry."

Think about a time when you were deeply troubled and distressed. Do you remember the words people said to you? Probably not. What you remember is the person who came and spent time with you, sharing your hurt. Compassion is caring in action. It's noticing a person's pain and lingering with them in the midst of their difficulties.

All around us, there are troubled people ready to call it quits. A simple compassionate act can help them put one foot in front of the other and move forward with their lives. They are family members, coworkers, and neighbors. Ask Jesus to give you missionary eyes to see the real trials of those you meet and to extend compassionate care to them. A helping hand can change the world, one heart, one life, at a time.

TAKEAWAY ROUTE: This Lent, be the compassionate friend who says, "I'm hurting with you…I'm standing with you…I'm crying with you. Take my hand and we'll get through this together."

TURN-IT-OVER ROUTE: *Jesus, help me take my eyes off myself so I can see what is going on in the lives of those around me. Amen.*

MARCH 11 | WEDNESDAY OF THE THIRD WEEK

Deuteronomy 4:1, 5–9 » Matthew 5:17–19

Watch out! You're contagious

"Whoever [keeps these commandments] and teaches them will be called great in the kingdom of heaven." Matthew 5:19

Pop star Demi Lovato told *Cosmopolitan* magazine, "When I was younger, I needed someone in the spotlight to idolize, who stood for positivity and light and happiness and wanted to change the world. And because I didn't have that, I realized I wanted to do that, if only for my twelve-year-old little sister."

Each of us carries the flu—not the disease kind, but the in-"flu"-ential kind. We will affect every person we come into contact with. Even if we're unaware, people will adopt certain mannerisms, catchphrases, and attitudes from us. The "flu" is contagious.

You're always communicating simply by being who you are, saying what you say, and doing what you do. You may be the only carrier of positive influence to another person.

When you're a healthy carrier of influence, you showcase absolute integrity, possess a positive frame of mind and attitude, deliberately listen, understand, and appreciate people's differences, and do what's right. You emphasize optimism, empathy, encouragement, and inspiration. The results? You experience a higher quality of life as you are healthier and feel good about yourself.

TAKEAWAY ROUTE: Draw a circle on paper and write: "My sphere of influence." Whom could you influence in a positive and powerful way? Write the names and determine specifically how you could positively affect their lives. Include these people in your prayers during Lent.

TURN-IT-OVER ROUTE: *Jesus, there's nothing more uplifting than knowing someone cared enough about me to influence me so well. Amen.*

MARCH 12 | THURSDAY OF THE THIRD WEEK

Jeremiah 7:23–28 » Luke 11:14–23

Arguments: the uninvited guest

"Whoever is not with me is against me." Luke 11:23

Every couple has the occasional heated debate, but some can escalate and quickly turn ugly, with name calling, silent treatment, or abandonment.

Before entering into a debate, figure out what you're going to say and how you're going to get your point across while avoiding a shouting match. Focus on the current issue and don't rehash a previous argument. Take ownership of your mistakes and apologize without making excuses.

Be careful that the things you say in the heat of anger won't be words you will later regret. Call a time-out if you have to. Leave the room and go for a walk. Regroup later, and have a mutually respectful conversation without spewing hurtful words. Recognize when things are simply unsolvable, and relinquish the need for the upper hand when you face a gridlock.

Once the issue is brought out in the open and thoroughly discussed, and a mutually agreed upon solution is reached, move forward. Keeping an argument alive will only bring further stress to the relationship.

TAKEAWAY ROUTE: When arguing, ask: What do you both need from the other during the dispute? Unearth the underlying issues.

TURN-IT-OVER ROUTE: *Jesus, when we resolve our disagreements, it reminds us why we are together—to grow in love, patience, respect, and forgiveness. Amen.*

MARCH 13 | FRIDAY OF THE THIRD WEEK

Hosea 14:2–10 » Mark 12:28–34

The treasure of you

"You shall love your neighbor as yourself."
Mark 12:31

"Always be a first-rate version of yourself, instead of a second-rate version of somebody else." This Judy Garland quote carries with it a time-honored moral: you have the right to be yourself. When you feel as if you don't measure up, you tend to compare and compete with others. You try to be somebody else.

As you look at other people's talents, you often put yourself down because you don't feel your talent measures up to theirs. The thing is, we all have things we can do and things we can't do. Stop thinking you're a nobody, and start believing you're a somebody whom God created to be fully you.

Each of us arrived in the world with a face, a voice, and a mind wholly unique. Discover this distinctiveness by creating a healthy atmosphere in which to grow. Lent is the perfect time to approve yourself with an awareness of "I am who I am and that's all I can be."

There will always be people who aren't satisfied with who we are. Let go of them. You can try to mold yourself to please others, but I guarantee they'll still find something wrong. The real you is far better than the you someone else creates.

TAKEAWAY ROUTE: The next time you pass a mirror, look at yourself and say to yourself: "You know it's true. There's only one you."

TURN-IT-OVER ROUTE: *Jesus, thanks for loving me just the way I am. I'm blessed. Amen.*

MARCH 14 | SATURDAY OF THE THIRD WEEK

Hosea 6:1–6 » Luke 18:9–14

The happily ever after of being wrong

"God, be merciful to me, a sinner." Luke 18:13

Have you ever been in the middle of a conversation when suddenly you realize you're dead wrong? Nothing is quite as frustrating as facing the dilemma of what to do. Instead of becoming defensive or trying to justify yourself, simply say, "I'm wrong."

Like the tax collector, I often pray: "God, I messed up." God's response? "So what? It's not the end of the world. The earth will still be in orbit and the mosquitoes will still bite."

God doesn't expect us to always be right. He'll never dismiss us or write us off because we have made whopper mistakes. However, he calls us to be responsible and not reckless and encourages us to open our eyes, admit our blunders, apologize, fix the problem, and avoid a repeat performance.

I've learned to live happily ever after with being wrong. It has taught me humility and in the process has released me from the illusion of perfection. Having the courage to say "I blew it" shows strength and character. It beats always having to be right! After all, none of us are flawless.

TAKEAWAY ROUTE: Take a deep breath, close your eyes, and whisper, "I was wrong." Repeat as many times as necessary. It's refreshing to admit we're flawed, reminding us that our shortcomings, once acknowledged, become stepping stones for growth and healing.

TURN-IT-OVER ROUTE: *Jesus, I own all the wrongs I've said or done. I sincerely desire to grow and change from these experiences. Amen.*

MARCH 15 | FOURTH SUNDAY OF LENT

2 Chronicles 36:14–16, 19–23 » Ephesians 2:4–10 » John 3:14–21
or (Year A) 1 Samuel 16:1b, 6–7, 10–13a » Ephesians 5:8–14 » John 9:1–41

The happiest place to be

"How did he open your eyes?" John 9:26

Kevin's doctors gave him only four months to live when he was diagnosed with stage two colon cancer. That was over three years ago. A single father of three teenage children, Kevin works full-time and receives chemotherapy every couple of weeks. He's often asked, "How do you live each day with cancer hanging over your head?" He smiles. "I treat every day as a gift," he says. "I refuse to get trapped looking backward or forward. I live for today." Then he adds, "I'm happier now than I was before I was diagnosed."

It's easy for us to waste our lives obsessing about petty concerns. By wandering into yesterday and worrying about tomorrow, we're passing on the only time we really have—today. We're missing out on the happiness we're chasing and the love we're yearning for.

Today is the most important day of your life. Live it now because it's disappearing quickly and will never come again. Enjoy the journey of the day, for this is the only day that is real right now. Dedicate yourself to it and watch the quality of your life rise through the roof!

TAKEAWAY ROUTE: Search for acoustic troubadour Jason Mraz's song "Living in the Moment," on YouTube. Watch it and listen to the words. It's a reminder that we have a limited time, so let's not throw it away.

TURN-IT-OVER ROUTE: *Jesus, you call yourself "I Am," not "I Was," or "I'm Gonna Be." Help me to live fully in the precious present—always. Amen.*

MARCH 16 | MONDAY OF THE FOURTH WEEK

Isaiah 65:17–21 » John 4:43–54

Let your words be few

The official said to him, "Sir, come down before my little boy dies."
John 4:49

"I won't have the joys of seeing him grow into adulthood, marry, and have a family of his own," a grieving mother told me after the funeral for her son. "That's all been taken away from me now."

Acknowledging the unimaginable loss of a child is one of the harshest things in life. What should, and what shouldn't, we say in a time like this?

Don't say, "I know exactly how you feel." You don't.

Don't say, "It was God's will," or "God must have needed another angel." There is no comfort in clichés.

Don't say, "It's time to get over it and move on with your life." Grief takes time.

Don't say, "Call me if there is anything I can do." They won't. Figure out what needs to be done and just do it. Run errands; clean, cook, and help in any way you can.

So what do you say? Not much. When hurt is fresh, our words should be few, but our actions should be plenty. Sometimes, all someone needs is your presence and a reassuring hug.

TAKEAWAY ROUTE: Grieving parents tend to become isolated when the crowd disappears and reality hits hard. Let them know you're there for them. Take them out to lunch or to a movie or invite them to your home. Even if they refuse, persist.

TURN-IT-OVER ROUTE: *Jesus, the death of a child is the worst nightmare for a parent. Give me the courage to be a caring presence to them. Amen.*

MARCH 17 | TUESDAY OF THE FOURTH WEEK

Ezekiel 47:1–9, 12 » John 5:1–16

The unexpected friend

"I have no one to put me into the pool."
John 5:7

Gretchen was understandably depressed after losing her job. While at a coffee shop, she saw a friend she hadn't spoken to in awhile. The friend noticed Gretchen was upset and asked, "What's going on?" Gretchen shared her situation and mentioned she was looking for work. Her friend made some suggestions, which Gretchen followed up on. Now she's happily employed.

We meet people for a reason. We all have steady friends who are always there, and revolving-door friends who come into our lives and soon depart. For thirty-eight years, our sick brother in the gospel was written off, treated like he was just part of the landscape. People passed him by or pushed him out of their way. Not Jesus. He stepped into his life and met his needs.

People walk into your life, and you know they're meant to be there to lift you up, teach you a lesson, listen when you need to talk, or help you figure out what you're supposed to do. You never know who they'll be—a neighbor, pastor, teacher, complete stranger, or a long lost friend. Once you establish eye contact, you know they were sent for a reason.

TAKEAWAY ROUTE: Reflect on this Flavia Weedn quote: "Some people come into our lives and quickly go. Some stay for awhile, leave footprints on our hearts, and we are never, ever the same."

TURN-IT-OVER ROUTE: *Jesus, I'm so blessed by those who perpetually stayed in my life when others permanently walked out. Amen.*

MARCH 18 | WEDNESDAY OF THE FOURTH WEEK

Isaiah 49:8–15 » John 5:17–30

What will we leave behind?

"Anyone who hears my word and believes…has eternal life."
JOHN 5:24

R.I.P. Rest in peace or rejoicing in paradise? For Christians, it's the latter—we've got a one-way ticket to enjoy everlasting life.

Heaven will be a spacious place with all sorts of treasures available to each of us. However, the entryway is too small for a U-Haul or armored car. We can't take anything with us to paradise. Nor do we need to. We'll just carry with us the love of those we've touched along our journey.

Once we enter heaven, we'll skip out on everything we didn't like on earth. No more plumbing problems, leaky roofs, houses to paint, lawn care, or broken refrigerators. No more windows to wash, snow to shovel, or dust bunnies to herd. Our heavenly home will be self-cleaning and complete with an eternal guarantee.

A wonderful life is awaiting us in heaven. No more struggling with difficulties or sinking in the spiritual doldrums. We'll be released from pain and problems, fears and frustrations, disappointments and discouragements—all the things that held us captive here on earth.

What we leave behind, besides the family heirlooms, are the stories, laughter, and hope shared with others. They'll never end up in a landfill but will live on in the hearts of family and friends forever.

TAKEAWAY ROUTE: At your next gathering, ask your family and friends how they'd want to be remembered if they died tomorrow.

TURN-IT-OVER ROUTE: *Jesus, I want my life spent on something that will outlast it. Amen.*

MARCH 19 | SOLEMNITY OF ST. JOSEPH

2 Samuel 7:4–5a, 12–14a, 16 » Romans 4:13, 16–18, 22 » Matthew 1:16, 18–21, 24a or Luke 2:41–51a

Destroying the what ifs

"Joseph, son of David, do not be afraid..."
Matthew 1:20

"Fear kicks in when I go to see my oncologist for blood work and other tests," a cancer survivor admitted, "but I'm not going to let it prevent me from enjoying life."

While fear is a normal emotion, we can't allow our lives to be controlled or immobilized by it. When the "what ifs..." raise their ugly heads, we give fear the power to rob us of experiencing joy, love, and other positive emotions. It's time to face your fears, take away their power, and change your "what if..." thinking to "I can handle this" thinking.

Look fear in the eyes, name it, and ask yourself two questions: "What is the worst-case scenario that can happen to me?" and "How will I deal with it?" Brainstorm positive steps you can take to face each of your fears. Write them down so you can see how your fears have become walls holding you back. Grab a sledgehammer and start hammering away, one fear at a time. When you recognize the progress you're making, your desire to stay at it will increase until each and every fear has vanished. Be realistic, but believe that, with God's help, you do have the strength and ability to handle anything.

TAKEAWAY ROUTE: Smash through your fears by doing what you've held off doing. Call about that new job. Look for a larger apartment. Meditate more often. Open up to that new relationship.

TURN-IT-OVER ROUTE: *Jesus, with your help, I can knock my fears down to size and handle them. Amen.*

MARCH 20 | FRIDAY OF THE FOURTH WEEK

WISDOM 2:1A, 12–22 » JOHN 7:1–2, 10, 25–30

Hide the goat

"You know me, and you know where I am from."
JOHN 7:28

"No one can get your goat if they don't know where it's tied up." This quote from Zig Ziglar applies perfectly to all those people who push your buttons at work, school, play, and home.

Be on the watch for the button-pushers: *Lethal Attackers* enjoy taking potshots at us through not-so-funny putdowns, disapproving looks, and cutting sarcasm. *Trash Pickers* love to collect behaviors and habits from our past and then throw them back in our face. *Snoopy Meddlers* stick their noses in our lives by offering unwelcome and unsolicited advice. *Instigators* are the typical schoolyard bullies barking accusations and ridicule. *Boastful Toppers* love to brag that they can do anything we do, only better.

We can lash out. Or use ACT steps to cut the wires.

Awareness. Name your button-pushers and identify their style. Figure out how to respond.

Choose an unexpected response. Stop before spewing fire. Are you overreacting to what was said/done?

Talk back to the button-pusher. "Enough. Keep pushing, but you're not getting the best of me."

People tried, unsuccessfully, to push Jesus' buttons. They walked away mumbling. Remember, once the buttons are deactivated, you reclaim the power to run your own life.

TAKEAWAY ROUTE: When someone tries to push your buttons, stay calm, then ACT.

TURN-IT-OVER ROUTE: *Jesus, I'm not going to let button-pushers prevent me from being who I am. Amen.*

MARCH 21 | SATURDAY OF THE FOURTH WEEK

JEREMIAH 11:18–20 » JOHN 7:40–53

Digging in your heels

So there was a division in the crowd because of him.
JOHN 7:43

"My husband loves action-adventure movies. He plops down in front of his wide-screen television with popcorn and soda and has a movie marathon," Marie said. "When I complain, he tells me to sit down and watch; I might like them."

I suggested that Marie and Dave compromise by alternating who gets to pick the movies. At first she hissed, "Are you kidding me?" But Dave said, "How 'bout we give it a try?" It worked.

How often do we dig our heels in and refuse to budge? Jesus ran into a brick wall when he encountered a crowd of "there's no way I am going to see it differently" attitudes over the origins of the Messiah.

A good compromise can smooth out the rough spots in our relationships. When couples come to an impasse, I ask, "Can you meet in the middle?" Even though one may feel completely right and that the other person is wrong, it just isn't worth fighting about.

Healthy compromise breaks the cycle of struggling to get the other to come around to your way of thinking. It opens the door to solving problems that may develop over how much time or money you're spending so that a deadlock happens less often. In the end, you'll both reap the benefits.

TAKEAWAY ROUTE: Be a phrase-dropper. Drop phrases like "That's just the way it is" or "Over my dead body." Work toward a healthy, livable compromise

TURN-IT-OVER ROUTE: *Jesus, turn me away from stubbornness and turn me towards openness. Amen.*

MARCH 22 | FIFTH SUNDAY OF LENT

Jeremiah 31:31–34 » Hebrews 5:7–9 » John 12:20–33
or (Year A) Ezekiel 37:12–14 » Romans 8:8–11 » John 11:1–45

Let it out

Jesus began to weep. John 11:35

His mother was on life support. "I have to be strong for my brother," my former student said, fighting back tears. "No, you don't," I told him. "It hurts. Get it out."

There is healing in crying, lamenting, sobbing, and wailing. Tears are gestures of compassion. A tear falling onto a casket speaks louder than words. Nothing summons more motherly attention and affection than a genuine tear on her child's cheek. Sympathy and support spill forth when we see tears on the face of a friend. Compassionate tears are the sign that we've taken the focus off ourselves and are really feeling with someone else.

Crying is not a sign of weakness. Real weakness emerges when we don't allow ourselves access to our emotions. Sadness and hurt don't disappear just because we refuse to cry. They are simply buried underground as our pain intensifies. Later, they show up in the form of stress, depression, and ulcers. Tears are on call 24/7 as miniature messengers when words fail. They fill uncomfortable moments and seep from our souls, bringing with them the deepest emotions we possess—from joy to pain. It's simple: when words are most elusive, tears are most appropriate.

TAKEAWAY ROUTE: Amanda Wilkinson's song "It's Okay to Cry" says it all, giving us permission to cry. Listen to the lyrics. Print them out and read them prayerfully. Then share them with someone who's known for holding back tears.

TURN-IT-OVER ROUTE: *Jesus, you're no stranger to crying. You understand the language of tears. Amen.*

MARCH 23 | MONDAY OF THE FIFTH WEEK

Daniel 13:1–9, 15–17, 19–30, 33–62 or 13:41c–62 » John 8:1–11

The uncast stone

"Has no one condemned you?" John 8:10

Shame, whether public or private, is always bitter. Without help, you'll never see the sunrise.

Your shame could be private—abuse by a parent, molestation from a relative, seduction by a superior. You're haunted by the fear of discovery.

Your shame could be public—an undeserved handicap, unwanted divorce, unexpected disease. Now you have to deal with being branded: invalid, divorcée, AIDS patient.

Crouched down in the center of the circle, a tearful, frightened woman is surrounded by an impassioned crowd, squeezing stones so tightly that their fingertips turn white. But there is a rescuer, one who stands out from the crowd. Jesus writes in the sand and as the shame-filled woman cowers, the only sound you hear is the thud of rocks dropping onto the ground and the shuffle of feet. Jesus and the woman are now alone, and he says, "not condemned."

Have you ever felt like the woman in this story? You made a mistake and felt the stares of people all around you. You sense the whispering behind your back. You wish you could hit rewind and make different choices, but you can't. What you can do is change, learn, grow, and live better. Jesus doesn't throw rocks. Instead, he offers a chance for true repentance.

TAKEAWAY ROUTE: Carry a stone in your pocket and keep it there as a reminder not to throw it at someone else. Follow Jesus' example.

TURN-IT-OVER ROUTE: *Jesus, when the crowd of finger-pointers disappears, I'm left with you alone, a forgiving friend. Amen.*

MARCH 24 | TUESDAY OF THE FIFTH WEEK

Numbers 21:4–9 » John 8:21–30

Mute your inner babble

As he was saying these things, many believed in him. John 8:30

I have a bumper sticker that says: "You Don't Have To Believe Everything You Say To Yourself." Most of us do, however. Our inner babble is either helpful—"I'm ready for this job interview"—or unhelpful—"I'm going to fail; there's no use trying." When you're feeling down, it's a good idea to keep an eye on your inner babble.

Maintain a distance from self-talk that compares, complains, comments, or criticizes others, yourself, or your life experiences. Unhelpful babble uses fear, doubt, and difficulty as its tactics to dissuade and discourage. It's a master in the art of persuasion, restricting your dreams and plans from taking off. Unhelpful babble fills your head with "stinkin' thinkin'" by taking a tiny blunder and inflating it into an epic typhoon of hopelessness.

Befriend helpful babble, which wants to encourage you to persist with what you normally resist. It's time to stop procrastinating, quitting too soon, or surrounding yourself with people who endorse the voices of negative self-talk.

While you can never totally eliminate unhelpful babble, you can minimize its voice of negativity and self-defeating chatter by hitting the mute button. Then maximize the helpful babble by cranking up the volume so that your conversations will be well thought out and your inner nays will become yays.

TAKEAWAY ROUTE: Wear a rubber band on your wrist and snap it every time unhelpful babble speaks up.

TURN-IT-OVER ROUTE: *Jesus, remind me that when I listen to unhelpful babble, it blocks me from hearing your gentle voice whisper words of encouragement. Amen.*

MARCH 25 | SOLEMNITY OF THE ANNUNCIATION

Isaiah 7:10–14; 8:10 » Hebrews 10:4–10 » Luke 1:26–38

If you can't beat them, join them

"Greetings, favored one! The Lord is with you." Luke 1:28

We all have a Debbie (or Dave) Downer in our lives—someone who exudes negativity, cynicism, and doom and gloom. There always seems to be a dark cloud raining misery into their lives, and they drain the joy out of life with their whining and complaining. Despite your best efforts to lead them in a positive direction, they refuse to follow. Even praying with them doesn't help. So, how do you move them out of their negativity nests?

If they want to rant, climb into their nest and rant with them. When they say, "I can't stand my life," respond with, "It must be hard for you." If they're moaning about a relationship, say, "I can't imagine how you're surviving all this pain."

By entering their negativity nest and ranting with them, you'll find them letting it go and moving away from their pessimism. They've been called out on their behavior, and their negativity is disarmed. By putting a mirror in front of them and not swimming against their stream of negativity, you help them transform their sour outlook into a sweet in-look. When they realize what they're missing, they'll decide it's time to leave the nest and stop being a victim.

TAKEAWAY ROUTE: Drop a quarter in a jar every time you speak a negative or cynical word/phrase/comment. After a year, donate the money to charity.

TURN-IT-OVER ROUTE: *Jesus, I see possibilities and not ends in each day. I look at all of life and affirm it is good...very good. Amen.*

MARCH 26 | THURSDAY OF THE FIFTH WEEK

Genesis 17:3–9 » John 8:51–59

Time for a conversation

"Abraham died, and so did the prophets; yet you say, 'Whoever keeps my word will never taste death.'" John 8:52

When my mother was dying, she and I talked about her end-of-life wishes. This treasured conversation is one I will always remember.

We rarely have conversations like this before crises hit. While we plan for a wedding, the birth of a child, college, and retirement, end-of-life conversations remain taboo.

As a hospital chaplain, I've seen families in turmoil because they failed to have this conversation with their parents or spouses and had no idea what their end-of-life wishes were.

Have this conversation with your family, sooner rather than later. Include your family physician, health care professionals, and your parish priest. Define what your loved one wants with a living will. Discuss hospice care and appoint a durable power of attorney for health and financial needs. Even funeral preparations should be made.

End-of-life wishes can be painful to discuss, but, despite its sensitivity, it's actually a caring gesture to ask, "What do you want?" Honor those you love by participating in the conversation.

TAKEAWAY ROUTE: Schedule an "end-of-life wishes conversation night" with your family. Discuss care, instructions for burial, and biographical information. Ensure the wishes are honored by distributing copies to everyone.

TURN-IT-OVER ROUTE: *Jesus, death is a blatant reminder to never postpone having the important talks with my family. Amen.*

MARCH 27 | FRIDAY OF THE FIFTH WEEK
JEREMIAH 20:10–13 » JOHN 10:31–42

Hedging or hugging?

"It is not for a good work that we are going to stone you, but for blasphemy." JOHN 10:33

Insecure in my early years in ministry, I used to lash out whenever I was criticized. Now, rather than getting defensive, I postpone my anger because, despite the hurt criticism imposes, it also is helpful. It helps me to improve.

We open ourselves up to critics every time we take a stand, and the criticism makes us feel vulnerable. We don't want to hear it when someone thinks we're doing things wrong or we need some kind of change. We feel we've failed.

If we expect and welcome the criticism, it won't catch us off guard when it hits. Hug it and don't hedge from it. Hedging causes us to avoid and turn a deaf ear to it, tempting us to even the score. Disapproval is perceived as a threat, so we slip into protector mode, dismissing the criticism and attacking the critics.

On the other hand, hugging the criticism offers comfort. Devoid of anger, excuses, or retaliation, huggers refuse to get emotionally hung up on it or to allow it permanent residence in their heads. They consider its value, recognize its truth, and then make any necessary adjustments in their life, relationships, or work.

TAKEAWAY ROUTE: Constructively handle criticism by making a commitment to be reflective. Stop and ask: is this going to help me improve? Is it reliable?

TURN-IT-OVER ROUTE: *Jesus, when I hear criticism, it feels like others are thinking less of me, when actually, they're thinking more because they want the best for me. Help me to hear and not be hostile. Amen.*

MARCH 28 | SATURDAY OF THE FIFTH WEEK

Ezekiel 37:21–28 » John 11:45–56

Still deliverable

Many of the Jews therefore, who had come with Mary and had seen what Jesus did, believed in him. JOHN 11:45

Anticipating my mom's recovery from open-heart surgery, I couldn't believe it when I heard the doctor say, "I did all I could. Your mom's heart was too weak. I'm sorry." *This must be a bad dream,* I thought. But it wasn't. Mom was dead.

I received a package the next day. Wrapped in tape, it was marked, "Damaged in transit but still deliverable." It reminded me that it's okay to feel unraveled. We're often damaged in transit. But Jesus says, "I know you've been damaged, but read the rest: 'still deliverable.'"

At times, the damage can seem too much to bear. An unfaithful spouse. The death of a child. Rape. We're cut to the core and feel as if we're the only ones who have ever been damaged this way. Veronica Roth writes: "Life damages us, every one. We can't escape that damage. But now I am also learning this: We can be mended. We mend each other."

If life has injured you, reach out to those around you; this is when healing begins. People do care and want to listen. Turn to a family member, loyal friend, support group, or suicide hotline. Allow yourself to be heard, understood, comforted. We're all damaged, but we're also all deliverable.

TAKEAWAY ROUTE: Damaged as we are, we are still loved. Connect with people and share your story in order to make sense out of your brokenness.

TURN-IT-OVER ROUTE: *Jesus, you hear my cries when I am damaged, and you help me to be deliverable again and again. Amen.*

MARCH 29 | PALM SUNDAY OF THE PASSION OF THE LORD

Mark 11:1–10 or John 12:12–16 » Isaiah 50:4–7 » Philippians 2:6–11
Mark 14:1—15:47

A tabloid tongue

Pilate asked him, "Are you the King of the Jews?"
He answered him, "You say so." Mark 15:2

The tabloids scream of it, and we laugh or shake our heads. But what about us? Is gossip a part of our lives too? Let's face it: gossip is enticing. We all want to know "the scoop." It's easy to fall into a pattern of repeating stuff that is only half true; stuff that can cause some real damage. And then we justify it by saying "other people need to know about this."

At one time or another, we've all found ourselves drawn to listening to the "dirt" about others. Hearing negative news about someone we know somehow makes us feel better about ourselves. "At least I'm not that bad." Yet, our tongue has the power to ruin a person's character and wound their spirit.

It's time to develop gossip-awareness with CTN.

Call people out when they start casting an unflattering light on someone.

Think before the words leave your mouth. Are they building a person up or tearing them down?

Never say something about someone that you wouldn't say to their face. Give them the chance to respond or just don't say it.

TAKEAWAY ROUTE: Memorize this: "Have you heard a negative word about your neighbor? Let it die within you." Then stay off Facebook, IM, and the phone. Be quiet.

TURN-IT-OVER ROUTE: *Jesus, help me to tame my tongue before it seriously injures someone. Amen.*

MARCH 30 | MONDAY OF HOLY WEEK

Isaiah 42:1–7 » John 12:1–11

Piquing your curiosity

When the great crowd of the Jews learned that he was there, they came not only because of Jesus but also to see Lazarus, whom he had raised from the dead. John 12:9

"I want to go someplace where I can marvel at something," Elizabeth Gilbert (Julia Roberts) says in the movie *Eat, Pray, Love*. Thus starts her life-changing journey through Italy, India, and Indonesia.

What about you? Do you marvel at your own life? Or is it spent surfing the web, watching TV, or spending hours in mindless activities? How much time is spent bonding with the people you love, talking with close friends, or simply playing?

Shake off the boring and invigorate your life with sheer curiosity. It's guaranteed to add wonder to your life and keep it fresh.

Curiosity is integral to making you feel alive with an eagerness to embrace greater opportunities, make deeper connections with others, and soak in all the simple pleasures life offers.

Live the curiosity-driven life. Pass your curiosity down to your children. Encourage them to question, wonder, and ponder more. Get excited when you discover something new. View God's creation through childlike eyes of awe and wonder—a leaf, a flower, winter snow, soft grass, rain, a sunrise, or a sunset. Savor those experiences that have piqued your curiosity. Life will never be the same.

TAKEAWAY ROUTE: Replace your busy schedule with curiosity days. Take in nature, read, meditate, or paint. There's a whole wide world waiting to be explored.

TURN-IT-OVER ROUTE: *Jesus, may I never lose my sense of curiosity. May there always be moments where I look at life and say, "Aha!" Amen.*

MARCH 31 | TUESDAY OF HOLY WEEK

Isaiah 49:1–6 » John 13:21–33, 36–38

Rx for the betrayal virus

"One of you will betray me." John 13:21

The e-mail revealed her husband's online affair with his old college girlfriend. "I trusted him completely," Joyce said. "I never imagined he'd betray me. How could have I been so naïve?"

None of us are immune to the betrayal virus. Like Joyce, you can collapse under the weight of it.

Jesus wasn't immune. The virus struck when Judas asked, "How much will you give me?" It struck again as Peter claimed, "I don't know him."

Surprisingly, Joyce set out to save her marriage. Do you want to know her prescription?

First, accept what happened and confront the betrayer in an effort to understand why he or she did it. If you simply sweep it under the carpet, you'll live in denial. Joyce didn't want that.

Next, express your feelings without holding anything back. If kept buried, they'll eventually arise and damage the relationship.

Finally, forgive. Joyce forgave Tom. It was difficult, but she didn't want to become a bitter woman.

Once she emptied her pain through forgiveness, healing began. Joyce and Tom can't return to the marriage they once had because those people are gone. But with time, patience, and hard work, they can build a new, stronger marriage.

TAKEAWAY ROUTE: If you're sickened by betrayal, follow Joyce's prescription. But be patient; healing takes time.

TURN-IT-OVER ROUTE: *Jesus, you were not immune to the betrayal virus; when I catch it, help me to trust again. Amen.*

APRIL 1 | WEDNESDAY OF HOLY WEEK

Isaiah 50:4–9a » Matthew 26:14–25

Family first

"I will keep the Passover...with my disciples."
Matthew 26:18

"Went fishing with my son today—day wasted!" Charles Francis Adams wrote this in his diary on the same day his son Brooks noted in his own diary, "Went fishing with my dad today—the most wonderful day of my life." Children never forget one-on-one time.

In our day-in, day-out lives, family time doesn't happen without effort. Putting family first means carving out time to be together. In order to feel more cohesive and less stretched as a family, try these starters:

Table time. It's important to partake in a daily ritual of gathering around the same table for a meal and sharing stories about your day. Set a place at the table for laughter and funny stories, as well as for planning family activities. Avoid indigestion by not welcoming problems or disciplinary matters at the table. If dinnertime doesn't work, aim for breakfast or lunch.

Family night in. Pop some popcorn and watch a movie. Read stories to each other. Go on a scavenger hunt. Put on a talent show. Make this a weekly or monthly routine where everyone stays home and participates.

It's the simplest activities that contribute to family bonding and long-term memories. And don't forget the goodnight hug and kiss!

TAKEAWAY ROUTE: Start a Family Home Evening. After dinner, go over family business, pray, or play together.

TURN-IT-OVER ROUTE: *Jesus, what's really needed at our dinner table is each other. Help me make my family a priority. Amen.*

APRIL 2 | HOLY THURSDAY

Exodus 12:1–8, 11–14 » 1 Corinthians 11:23–26 » John 13:1–15

Calling all designated hitters

"You also ought to wash one another's feet."
John 13:14

"Dad often finds it difficult to understand what people are saying, and he constantly repeats himself," a woman told me, explaining how overwhelmed her mom feels as her dad's Alzheimer's progresses. Her mom gains strength from those who stand alongside her. She and her brothers take him to his doctor's appointments. Parish members visit regularly. Some take him out for a ride, play cards, or go bowling. They all lend her mom the courage to go on.

There are everyday heartaches: illnesses, financial woes, being bullied, or feeling unappreciated. Then there are the more serious heartaches: an inoperable tumor, dissolution of marriage, an unwed daughter who's pregnant, or a family member with Alzheimer's.

We all face those moments when life pitches us heartaches. That's when we need a DEH on our team. The Designated Encourager Hitter can step up to the plate for us and hit it out of the ballpark, reminding us we're not alone.

As we gather tonight to wash and eat, Jesus gently nudges us to leave our churches and immerse ourselves into the lives of people needing an encouraging word. Your encouragement might keep someone from giving up on life. It may lead them to Jesus. We'll never really know how far a word of encouragement will reach until we make the effort.

TAKEAWAY ROUTE: Assign yourself as a DEH to someone who needs uplifting—a lonely neighbor, upset friend, or homebound relative.

TURN-IT-OVER ROUTE: *Jesus, I want to be a shoulder to lean on so others don't fall down. Amen.*

APRIL 3 | GOOD FRIDAY

Isaiah 52:13—53:12 » Hebrews 4:14–16; 5:7–9 » John 18:1—19:42

Breaking the holding pattern

Then he bowed his head and gave up his spirit. John 19:30

"Ah yes, the past can hurt," Rafki tells Simba in *The Lion King*. "But the way I see it, you can either run from it or learn from it."

I get that people are hurt and angry, and often with good reason. But playing the "blame game" won't get them anywhere. "You did this…" "I'm still mad at you because…" "Remember when you…" On and on it goes. Embracing past hurts and pains is tiresome, and it affects our health, relationships, and self-esteem.

Invite Jesus in. He doesn't say, "Get your act together first." Rather, he says, "Let me in your life and I'll help you clean up the wreckage of your past so you can walk bravely into today." When Jesus starts this inner work, don't interfere. Let him break the chains of guilt, anger, regret, and bitterness and set you free.

As much as you don't want to hear it, the world keeps turning and all the people who have hurt you have moved on or died. There will never be a time when life is simple. Every moment is a chance to let go and move out of the holding pattern that's shortchanging your life. Today, step forward and let go of what's in the past.

TAKEAWAY ROUTE: Let the past pass by writing down all you want to let go of. Then bury it in the yard and forget about it.

TURN-IT-OVER ROUTE: *Jesus, I need your help to shut and lock the door of my past permanently. Amen.*

APRIL 4 | HOLY SATURDAY (EASTER VIGIL)

Genesis 1:1—2:2 or 1:1, 26-31a » Genesis 22:1-18 or 22:1-2, 9a, 10-13, 15-18
Exodus 14:15—15:1 » Isaiah 54:5–14 » Isaiah 55:1–11 » Baruch 3:9–15, 32—4:4
Ezekiel 36:16–17a, 18–28 » Romans 6:3–11 » Mark 16:1–7

Live off your passion

"He has been raised; he is not here." Mark 16:6

A US Airways jet struck a flock of geese during its initial climb, losing engine power and ditching into the Hudson River off midtown Manhattan. Thanks to Captain Sullenberger, all 155 passengers survived. A reporter asked one passenger about his experience. Standing there soaking wet and freezing cold, the passenger glowed. With excitement in his voice, he said, "I was alive before, but now I'm really alive."

LIFE—it's an acronym for Live It Fully Everyday. Jesus calls us to do more than just go through the motions. He wants us to snap up life with passion. Grab hold of it and don't let go!

To recapture passion, start to live your life and own your choices. Do something you enjoy. Nurture your talents. Choose to see the good in people and love them. When life hits hard—stop, adapt, and move on. Sprinkle your life with adventures. If you fail at something, leave it behind and adjust. Don't put off passionate living. Do it today! Happy Easter!

TAKEAWAY ROUTE: Easter challenges us to ask, "Are you passionate about the life God has given you? Do you wake up every morning filled with purpose, exhilarated about the chance of another twenty-four hours on earth?" Share these questions with family and friends.

TURN-IT-OVER ROUTE: *Jesus, thank you for giving me the gift of this beautifully wrapped day. I know it's just waiting for me to open it and live it. Amen.*

Living with Christ
THE WORD OF GOD, DAILY PRAYER & THE BREAD OF LIFE

Designed to be every Catholic's guide to praying and living the Eucharist

Subscribe to *Living with Christ* and you will have an endless resource at your fingertips each and every month, all month long, including:

- A prayer from the Saints for each day
- The daily Mass readings
- A daily reflection on the readings
- The Pope's prayer intentions
- Additional faith-filled articles written by award-winning contributors

WHETHER IN CHURCH OR AT HOME, LET *LIVING WITH CHRIST* GUIDE YOU ON YOUR SPIRITUAL JOURNEY EACH AND EVERY DAY.

This edition is based on the American Lectionary.

✓ Yes! Start my subscription to ***Living with Christ***. I'll receive 12 issues Plus the special Holy Week edition for just $24.95.

☐ Check enclosed   ☐ Please bill me later
☐ Charge my: ○ Visa   ○ MasterCard   ○ Discover   ○ AMEX

Card # _____ Exp. date _____

Signature _____

Name *(please print)* _____

Address _____

City _____ State _____ Zip _____

Phone _____ Email _____

OFFER EXPIRES SEPT 30, 2015   (CODE) 51500LT1

Mail completed order form to

LIVING WITH CHRIST ■ PO BOX 293040 ■ KETTERING, OH 45429
WWW.LIVINGWITHCHRIST.US ■ **CALL 1-800-214-3786**

★ *Bulk discounts available* (3+ copies to one address)